WHY CHARLES GOODNIGHT MATTERS TO TEXAS

By Lynn Peppas

Published in 2014 by The Rosen Publishing Group, Inc.
29 East 21st Street, New York, NY 10010

Copyright © 2014 by Digital Discovery Publishing

All rights reserved. No part of this book may be reproduced in any form without permission in writing from the publisher, except by a reviewer.

First Edition

Developed, written, and produced by Digital Discovery Publishing
Editors: Molly Aloian, Wendy Scavuzzo
Design & Production: Katherine Berti
Curriculum & Content Coordinator: Reagan Miller
Photo research: Crystal Sikkens, Allison Napier
Proofreader: Sarah Cairns
Consultant: Dr. Tim Chandler, Director Media Production, Hardin-Simmons University, Department of Communications

Photo Credits: Amarillo Globe-News: 30
Armstrong County Museum: 4, 20, 23, 24, 26 (top), 27 (bottom), 29 (top right, middle)
Peter Newark American Pictures/Bridgeman Art Library: 1
Courtesy of the Burton Historical Collection/Detroit Public Library: 18 (bottom)
Getty Images/James P. Blair/National Geographic: 16 (bottom)
The Granger Collection, NYC: 10, 11 (bottom), 15, 19, 25
North Wind Picture Archives: 7 (top)
Panhandle-Plains Historical Museum, Canyon, Texas: 21, 23
Shutterstock: 3, 7 (top), 16, 27 (top)
The Image Works: 11 (top); © Mary Evans Picture Library: 8, 9 (bottom)
Texasarchive.org: 25
Wikimedia Commons: cover, 9 (top), 13, 14, 15, 16 (top), 17, 28, 29 (bottom)
Maps by Digital Discovery Publishing: 5, 6, 12, 14

All websites were live and accurate at the time of printing.

Library of Congress Cataloging-in-Publication Data

Peppas, Lynn.
Why Charles Goodnight matters to Texas / by Lynn Peppas.
   p. cm. – (Texas perspectives)
Includes index.
ISBN 978-1-4777-0907-8 (library binding) – ISBN 978-1-4777-0918-4 (pbk.) – ISBN 978-1-4777-0919-1 (6-pack)
1. Goodnight, Charles, 1836-1929 – Juvenile literature. 2. Cowboys – Texas – Biography – Juvenile literature. 2. Pioneers – Texas – Biography – Juvenile literature. 3. Frontier and pioneer life – Texas – Juvenile literature. I. Peppas, Lynn. II. Title.
F391.G66 P47 2013
976.4–dc23

Manufactured in the United States of America

CPSIA Compliance Information: Batch W13PK: For Further Information contact Rosen Publishing, New York, New York at 1-800-237-9932

CONTENTS

Chapter 1 . . . . . **Trailblazer!** 4

Chapter 2 . . . . . **Early Years** 6

Chapter 3 . . . . . **Cattle Drives** 10

Chapter 4 . . . . . **Ranching** 16

Chapter 5 . . . . . **Cattle King** 21

Chapter 6 . . . . . **Charles's Legacy** 28

Learning More 30

Timeline 31

Glossary 32

Index 32

1 TRAILBLAZER!

Charles Goodnight was **30** years old in **1866** when he decided to **blaze**, or mark out, a new trail to Denver, Colorado. Charles was in search of a market to sell his cattle, but there were many dangers ahead. Horse and cattle thieves, Indians, poisonous ponds, and long stretches without fresh water could easily turn a successful drive into a disaster. Charles made the trail, though, and became one of the first cattlemen to settle in the Llano Estacado, or Staked Plain, area of Texas.

CATTLEMAN

Charles was an outdoorsman who loved nature. He was also a smart businessman. Charles chose to drive his cattle through some of the harshest lands in Texas. It was a tough trail to blaze, but Charles and his cattle made it to Colorado when others might not have.

Charles Goodnight became one of the most successful "cattle kings" in Texas.

From an unpublished account about the area in Texas that Charles and Oliver Loving blazed:

> *At that time the Pecos was the most desolate country that I had ever explored. The river was full of fish, but besides the fish there was scarcely a living thing, not even wolves or birds.*

Charles Goodnight explored some of the most deserted areas in northwestern Texas. He also started one of the most profitable cattle ranches in the Texas Panhandle area. Charles knew more about the landscape of Texas and the animals that lived there than anyone else. He even bred new species of cattle that were stronger and could survive the long drives in the dry, desert areas of Texas.

Texas Perspective

In 1866 Charles Goodnight blazed the Goodnight-Loving Trail with Oliver Loving. It was a longer, safer route to drive cattle to market.

GOODNIGHT'S TEXAS

Locations shown on map:
- Canadian River
- Goodnight
- JA Ranch, Palo Duro Canyon
- Palo Duro Canyon
- Quitaque Ranch, Quitaque
- Caprock Canyons
- Llano Estacado
- Red River
- Brazos River
- Black Springs Ranch, Palo Pinto County
- TEXAS
- Colorado River
- Pecos River
- Middle Concho River

United States

2 EARLY YEARS

Charles Goodnight was born on March 5, 1836, in Macoupin County, Illinois. Charles was named after his father. After his father died of pneumonia in 1841, Charles's mother, Charlotte, married a farmer named Hiram Daugherty.

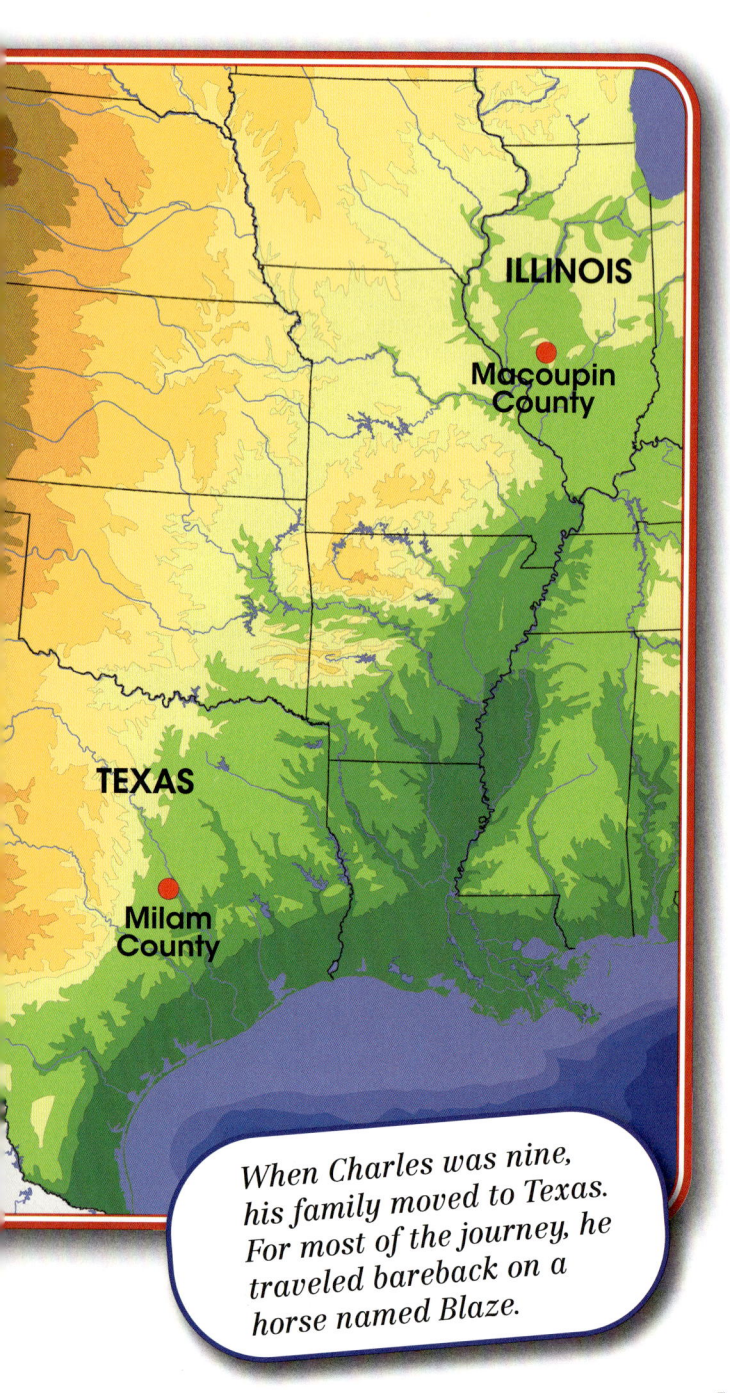

CHILDHOOD

Charles was a very observant child. He loved nature and spent a lot of time outdoors. He began school at age seven but had to quit after just six months. In 1845, Charles and his family moved to Milam County, Texas, near the Brazos River. On the journey to Texas, Charles saw a buffalo, or bison, for the first time. He watched dogs hunt the bison. Charles soon learned how to hunt and track animals from an Indian named Caddo Jake.

When Charles was 11, his mother had another baby and left her husband. Charles and his older brother Elijah had to find work to support the family. They moved to Port Sullivan in 1848. He and his brother caught a **mustang**. Charles helped to break the wild horse so they could ride it. At age 15, he became a jockey and raced horses. Charles went on to become one of the best horseback riders in Texas.

When Charles was nine, his family moved to Texas. For most of the journey, he traveled bareback on a horse named Blaze.

BLACK SPRINGS RANCH

In 1853, Charles's mother married a preacher named Adam Sheek. Three years later, Charles went into the cattle business with his stepbrother John Wesley Sheek. Charles and John began raising and caring for cattle together. Charles also delivered goods, such as cotton. He drove a team of oxen to pull large loads of goods throughout Texas. In 1857, Charles and John moved their herd and families to Palo Pinto County. They settled there and created the Black Springs Ranch.

HISTORY OF TEXAS RANCHING

The tradition of herding cows on horseback began in Europe. The Spanish word for "cowhands" is *vaqueros*. The Spanish arrived in Mexico in 1521 and claimed the land for Spain. They called the area New Spain. The Spaniards brought horses and cattle to the area. They also introduced their cattle-raising methods of farming to the native Mexican people. The Spanish settled in areas of Texas in the 1600s, bringing their ranching traditions with them. The cattle the Spaniards first brought to America were called Criollo cattle. These cattle were bred with cattle from other parts of Europe and Great Britain. This new breed of cattle is known as Texas longhorn cattle.

*Texas longhorns were hardy animals that could survive in the rugged Texas **terrain**.*

The Spanish introduced the practice of herding cows on horseback to North America.

PLAINSMAN AND SCOUT

Over the years, Charles became a skilled plainsman. A plainsman is a person who knows how to travel throughout, and survive in, the harsh plains of northwestern Texas. In 1857, Charles joined the Texas Rangers as a scout and guide. As a scout, he had to ride ahead of the Texas Rangers to warn the company of surprise attacks from Indians. At that time, the Texas **frontier**, especially the plains area, was a vast wilderness with no maps, marked roads, or pathways.

Charles explained his job as scout in the following way:

" It was a scout's business to guide the company under all conditions. Thus, above all things, the scout and plainsman had to have a sense—an instinct—for direction....I never had a compass in my life. I was never lost. In all my frontier experience, I knew but one man who had keener senses than I had. He was a Tonkawa Indian and his eyesight would carry farther than mine. "

TEXAS RANGERS

Groups of Indians, such as the Comanche, sometimes attacked settlers in the Texas area. In 1823, Stephen Austin formed the Texas Rangers. Their job was to enforce the law, act as scouts, help find stolen cattle and horses, protect settlers from attacks, fight in wars against Mexican or Indian forces, and carry messages on the Texas frontier.

◀ *The Texas Rangers patrolled on horseback and carried guns.*

CYNTHIA ANN PARKER

In 1860, Comanche Indians were believed to have attacked and killed a number of farming families throughout Texas. Charles was working with the Texas Rangers, and he successfully tracked the Comanche and led the Rangers to Comanche chief Peta Nocona's camp. The Rangers attacked and many Indians were killed. After the battle, the Rangers discovered that Peta Nocona's wife was a woman named Cynthia Ann Parker. She had been **kidnapped** by Indians when she was a child.

By the time she was rescued, Cynthia Ann had adopted the Comanche ways of life and did not want to leave. She tried to escape from the Texas Rangers.

TEXAS NATIONAL GUARD

On April 12, 1861, the Civil War began. The Civil War was a conflict that divided the United States into two opposing armies. The Northern states were called the Union, and the Southern states were called the Confederacy. Texas joined the Confederacy. The government of Texas organized a force called the Texas National Guard to patrol and protect the wilderness frontiers during the war. Charles volunteered and joined the force. The Texas National Guard protected the Texas frontier from attacks by Indians, Mexicans, Union soldiers, and Texans loyal to the Union.

Charles worked for the Texas National Guard until the spring of 1864. He then returned to his home in Palo Pinto County. In April 1865 the Civil War ended. The Union had won.

3 CATTLE DRIVES

In 1866, Charles Goodnight returned to the **Black Springs Ranch** to find that most of his cattle had been stolen while he was in service during the Civil War. The war had been long and difficult. Times were tough for cattle owners and other citizens.

BRANDING

Cattle in Texas were ranged, or allowed to move about freely over large areas. Cattle owners **branded** or **earmarked** their cattle. The cattle were kept together within boundaries by hired hands called cowboys or cowmen. Many cowboys or cowmen were fighting in the Civil War, so there was no one to keep the cattle together. Charles, like most other cowmen at the time, was not home to brand any newly born calves. Indians and outlaw cowmen, or rustlers, stole Charles's unbranded herd. Charles estimated that he would have a herd of 5,000, but he returned home to find only about 1,000 left.

Branding is a type of tattoo burned onto the tough skin of cattle. Earmarks were special patterns cut out of the ears of animals.

OLIVER LOVING

Charles met Oliver Loving around 1857 when Charles first settled at the Black Springs Ranch. Loving owned a small country store and a herd of cattle nearby. Loving was an experienced cowman. He drove cattle for hundreds of miles (km) east to sell in the states of Louisiana or Mississippi. He also drove cattle north to sell in other states such as Illinois and Colorado.

When Charles returned to his ranch after the Civil War, he was 30 years old. He began his first cattle drive in 1866. Charles decided to drive his cattle northwest because many southerners were **bankrupt** from the war and did not have money to buy cattle.

Oliver Loving was a pioneer cattle driver who owned approximately 1,000 acres (405 ha) of land.

Texas Perspective

Charles crossbred different kinds of cattle to create a breed that was tough enough to survive on the harsh Texas plains.

It was common for cattle to be driven across streams and other waterways.

DANGERS OF THE TRAIL

Working for the Texas Rangers taught Charles a lot about the dangers of the Texas frontier. He knew that if he drove his cattle in a direct line northwest to Colorado, the Kiowa or Comanche might steal his herd and possibly kill him. For that reason, Charles blazed a new trail. It was almost twice as long, but safer. The new route involved a long journey through dry, desertlike terrain. Charles planned to drive his cattle southwest to the Pecos River at Horsehead Crossing. He would then head to Denver, Colorado, by following the Pecos River and heading northward along the Rocky Mountains through parts of Texas and New Mexico. As Charles started his cattle drive, he met up with Oliver Loving. Loving warned Charles about driving the cattle across long stretches of dry land. Charles was still determined to go, and Loving asked to come along. Charles agreed, and on June 6, 1866, the two men, along with 18 other cowmen, moved a herd of 2,000 cattle across Texas. Their trail became known as the Goodnight-Loving Trail.

This map shows the route of the Goodnight-Loving Trail.

TRAIL TROUBLES

Just as Loving warned, the trail was hard on the men and cattle. Charles rode about 12 miles (19 km) ahead to search for water holes or a place to set up camp. They stopped at the Middle Concho River to let the herd drink before the next 80 miles (129 km) to the Pecos River.

The cowmen drove the thirsty cattle for three days. Almost 300 cattle died of thirst during the drive. Charles knew that the herd's extreme thirst could be dangerous. He did not want the herd drinking from poisonous water holes or ponds near the Pecos River. Charles's knowldge of the Texas landscape allowed him to guide the large herd of cattle toward the river in a safe manner.

J. Evetts Haley refers to Charles's experience in his book, called *Charles Goodnight: Cowman and Plainsman:*

> *There was an alkali pond near the river which would have meant death to [the cattle], but by pulling a few hairs from my horse's neck and letting them float to the ground, I detected the exact course of the breeze and took advantage of it, so that when the cattle smelled the water, they would strike for the ford of the river instead of the pond.*

LLANO ESTACADO

Llano Estacado is a plains region in southwestern Texas. It is also known as the Staked Plain. It got this name because travelers used stakes, or pointed pieces of wood, to locate watering holes and keep moving forward in a straight direction. Llano Estacado is the southernmost tip of the Great Plains region of North America. It lies south of the Canadian River in the northwest of Texas and northeast of New Mexico. It is one of the largest tablelands in North America and covers about 30,000 square miles (78,000 sq km) of land. It has a very dry, desert climate.

Llano Estacado is covered in short grasses that rise into one of North America's largest tabletop mesas. Mesas are hills with flat tops and steep sides.

THE CHUCK WAGON

In the untamed west, places to buy food were few and far between. Cowmen had to carry and prepare their own food, which they called "chuck," when they were on cattle drives. Chuck often consisted of coffee, bacon, and hard biscuits in a bag, carried behind a saddle. For longer cattle drives, more provisions were packed and carried on mules.

Charles Goodnight changed how cowmen ate on the trail when he created the first chuck wagon. Goodnight remodeled a wagon that could be pulled by oxen or mules. He added a chuck box, which was a hinged lid that rested on a swinging leg, to the back of the wagon. The lid became a table to cook and work on. The wagon carried provisions such as water, utensils, and a sourdough keg. A hired cook prepared foods such as beef, beans, stews, and sourdough biscuits. It was a big improvement over the meals that most cowmen were used to on the trail.

There was a spot for firewood underneath the chuck wagon. Small items were kept on shelves or in drawers in the chuck box.

PARTNERS TO THE END

Charles Goodnight and Oliver Loving trusted each other and worked well together on the trail. They decided to form a partnership for buying and selling cattle. In 1867, the partners were moving cattle when they were attacked by a group of Indians. The Indians stole about 200 cattle. Shortly after, Loving decided to leave the cattle under Charles's care so he and another cowman could hurry to Sante Fe to make a business deal. Charles tried to talk Loving out of leaving. Charles knew it was a very dangerous idea with so many Indians nearby.

The Comanche were skilled at fighting on horseback. Warfare was an important part of their lifestyle.

UNDER SIEGE

Unfortunately, Loving and the other cowman, Bill Wilson, did not listen to Charles's advice. The two cowmen set out in broad daylight, and a group of Comanche attacked. At one point, Wilson tried to talk to the Comanche, but during the effort Loving was shot in the wrist and side. The Comanche held the men under **siege** for days. Loving thought he might die from his injuries, so the two men formed a plan for Wilson to escape, go back to Charles, and return with help. Loving bravely fought off the Indian attacks for two days without food or sleep. On the third day, he made his own escape. Days later, travelers found him. They fed him and took him to Fort Sumner, in New Mexico, which was about 250 miles (402 km) away.

Charles found Loving at Fort Sumner, but his friend and business partner was not doing well. Loving got **gangrene** in his wounded arm, and a doctor at Fort Sumner **amputated** it. Loving survived the operation but died shortly after on September 25, 1867. Before he died, Charles promised Loving that he would find a way to bury him in Texas.

J. Evetts Haley references Charles's recommendation to travel only at night:

> *I assured [Loving] that it would be safe enough for him to go if he would travel only at night and hide out during the daytime, selecting his stops with a view of defense.*

Texas Perspective

Charles Goodnight invented the chuck wagon to feed his ranch hands on long cattle drives.

15

4 RANCHING

In 1869, Charles Goodnight started the Rock Canyon Ranch in Pueblo, Colorado. He traveled to Kentucky the next year and married Mary Ann (Molly) Dyer on July 26, 1870. Charles brought his new wife and her two younger brothers, Walter and Samuel, back to Colorado. Charles moved back to Texas in 1876 and staked a claim of land for a ranch in the Palo Duro Canyon, in the Texas Panhandle.

JOHN ADAIR

John Adair was a wealthy businessman from the United Kingdom. He moved to New York in 1866 and married his wife, Cornelia, in 1869. In 1874, the couple went to Nebraska for a buffalo hunt. They decided to move to the area and start a cattle ranch in Texas. In 1876, Charles Goodnight received a loan from Adair. Adair had heard about Charles's reputation as a cowman and rancher. Adair offered to partner with Charles to start a ranch in the Texas Panhandle. Charles agreed, and on June 18, 1877, Adair put up the money for the land and operations and Charles agreed to manage it for five years. They called it the JA Ranch.

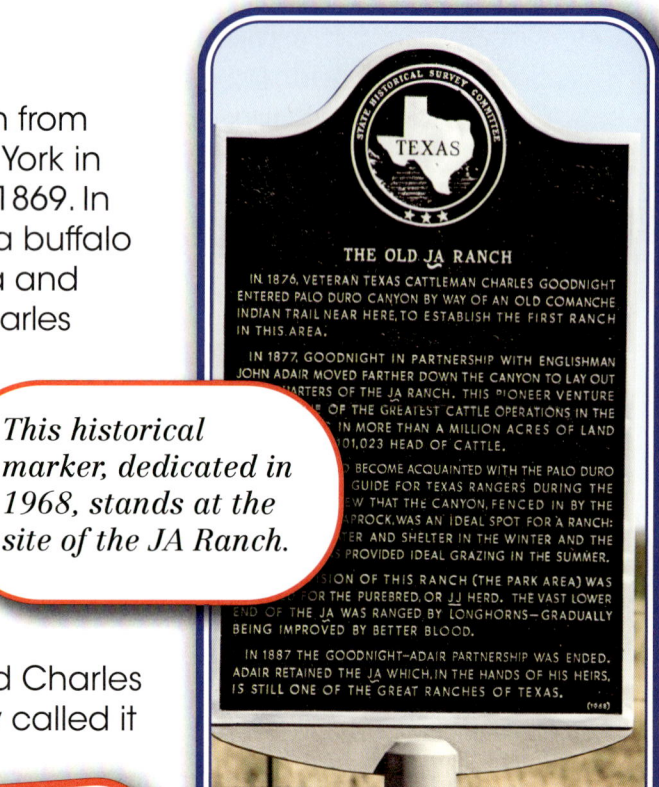

This historical marker, dedicated in 1968, stands at the site of the JA Ranch.

◀ These American buffalo are traveling to find food. Charles Goodnight had the idea to crossbreed buffalo and cattle to create a strong new animal called the catallo.

Today, JA Ranch is owned and operated by the Richie family, who are descendants of Cornelia Adair.

JA RANCH

As Charles and John Adair were building the JA Ranch, other cowmen were also moving to the Texas Panhandle area to start up new ranches. New towns were established including Mobeetie, Clarendon, and Tascosa. These towns still exist. Today, the JA Ranch is the oldest privately owned cattle ranch in the Texas Panhandle. Charles used his skills and knowledge as a rancher to build the JA Ranch up to over one million acres (404,686 ha) of land and more than 100,000 cattle.

CORNELIA ADAIR

The "JA" in JA Ranch stands for John Adair's initials. This is the brand they used to mark their cattle.

Cornelia Adair was born in 1837. She became a skilled horse rider and hunter as a young girl growing up in Gennessee Valley, New York. Cornelia loved the outdoors and once rode 400 miles (644 km) from Colorado to Texas on horseback. She also took part in roundups on the ranch. After her husband died in 1885, Cornelia continued to successfully run the JA Ranch.

BREEDING BETTER CATTLE

Charles knew that different breeds of cattle had different advantages over others for life in the Great Plains. For instance, Charles praised the Texas longhorn cattle for their ability to be driven long distances on trails. During his time managing the JA Ranch, Charles began trying to **crossbreed** different breeds of cattle to produce stronger, hardier, and heavier cattle that could survive on the plains and make good beef. Some of the cowmen who had moved to the Texas Panhandle from Colorado brought a shorthorn breed of cattle to the area. Charles bought some shorthorn cattle.

NEAR EXTINCTION

Before the 1850s, millions of wild buffalo roamed the Plains area of Texas and the United States. In the 1870s, the US government encouraged the **slaughter**, or killing, of large numbers of wild buffalo. The government wanted to save grazing lands for farmed animals. They also wanted to clear buffalo from railroad tracks. Americans often hunted buffalo for their skins, which they used for rugs, clothing, and machine belts for industries. They also sold the skins to Europeans. Indians relied on the buffalo for food, shelter, and clothing.

◀ *This picture shows an enormous pile of buffalo skulls. During the late 1800s, buffalo were hunted almost to extinction.*

The buffalo population quickly diminished when Americans began shooting herds alongside train tracks.

Charles Goodnight on the Texas longhorn breed:

> As trail cattle [Texas longhorns'] equal has never been known and never will be....They can go farther without water and endure more suffering than others....They have less tendency to lose weight in trailing; thus it does not require near as much skill and patience to handle them on the trail as it does the blooded races. From my observation they have at least double the endurance, and their period of life and usefulness is also about double that of any other.

QUANAH PARKER

In 1878, Comanche Indians came to hunt the near-extinct buffalo in the Palo Duro Canyon area of Texas. Charles knew the Indians would steal his cattle if they could not find enough buffalo to feed their people. Charles made a **treaty** with Comanche leader Quanah Parker. The treaty allowed the Indians to kill two cattle every day to feed themselves until they could find buffalo to hunt. The treaty kept peace among the Panhandle ranchers and Indians.

CATTALO

Charles recognized the wild buffalo as an animal that was even hardier than the Texas longhorn. He and his wife, Molly, began to raise their own herd of buffalo. Charles wanted to find out if he could cross buffalo with Polled Angus cows, so he crossbred the two to produce cattalo.

Quanah Parker was the son of Cynthia Ann Parker, whom Charles Goodnight had rescued many years before.

Although difficult to breed, a small number of cattalo are still bred in Canada today.

CATTLE KING

Charles Goodnight fulfilled his contract on the JA Ranch in 1887. Upon leaving, Charles received the Quitaque Ranch property. He also purchased another ranch known as the Goodnight Ranch in Armstrong County, Texas. He raised buffalo and kept other wild animals such as elk, antelope, deer, and birds on the ranch.

MOLLY GOODNIGHT

Mary Ann (Molly) Dyer, Charles's wife, was born in Tennessee on September 12, 1830. Her family moved to Fort Belknap, Texas, in 1854. In 1860, she taught school in Weatherford, Texas, even though she never went to college and had been educated by her parents at home. By 1866, Molly's parents were both dead and she took on the responsibility of raising her younger brothers, Samuel and Walter. When Charles and Molly first settled in Palo Duro Canyon, in 1877, Molly cared for her husband, her brothers, and the many cowhands who helped on the JA Ranch. She even nursed those who fell ill back to health.

Texas Perspective

Charles helped form the Panhandle Stock Association to protect cowmen and their cattle from rustlers.

▲ *After her marriage to Charles Goodnight, Molly was often called the Mother of the Plains.*

CONSERVATION

Molly, like Charles, was interested in nature and ranching. She was a skilled horse rider, and she sometimes accompanied her husband on cattle drives. By the late 1800s, the buffalo population was quickly decreasing. At Molly's request, Charles brought her abandoned buffalo calves to care for. Other neighbors also brought her buffalo calves. Molly started and cared for her own herd of Southern Plains buffalo. When the buffalo became dangerously close to extinction, her herd flourished and kept the breed going.

Goodnight Ranch was a major attraction for tourists. It featured 250 buffalo, other wild animals and birds, and Goodnight's two-story ranch home, complete with indoor bathrooms and roofed porches.

THE WILD, WILD WEST

Charles and other ranchers and settlers had to overcome all kinds of hardships in the Texas Panhandle. For example, there was no organized legal system in the Panhandle. Many people had to fend for themselves against thieves and rustlers, who often stole cattle to sell in other states. Outbreaks of Texas fever, a **fatal** disease that affected certain breeds of cattle, were another big problem. Panhandle ranchers were constantly worried that their cattle herds would catch the disease and die.

PANHANDLE STOCK ASSOCIATION

To help create order in the Panhandle, Charles created a group called the Panhandle Stock Association (PSA). In March of 1880, the Panhandle ranchers elected Charles as the president of the organization. The PSA created laws and punished wrongdoers in the Panhandle. The PSA also built a large fence to help keep diseased cattle away from healthy herds. It paid to have a doctor move to the Clarendon area to provide health care. Under Charles's direction, the organization also gave money to start the Panhandle's first public school in 1882. By 1885, many rustlers and thieves had moved on to other locations.

GOODNIGHT COLLEGE

In 1890, Charles sold the Quitaque Ranch. He put his money into a gold and silver mine in Mexico, but it was not successful and Charles lost a lot of money. Charles and Molly opened the Goodnight College in 1898. Charles gave the school 340 acres (138 ha) of land. Students who could not afford **tuition** were able to work at the school to help raise cattle and tend food crops. The school focused on teaching its students how to live on the Llano Estacado. Many of the students were children who grew up on nearby ranches. Molly helped care for the students of the college. Other colleges soon opened nearby, though, and the school closed in 1917.

Molly Goodnight played a major role in getting Goodnight College started. She invited the college students out to the Goodnight house regularly.

SILVER SCREEN

In 1916, Charles staged a buffalo hunt for Kiowa and Comanche Indians. Two filmmakers from Denver, Colorado, filmed the hunt. The movie they made was called *Old Texas*, and it was one of the first films made in Texas.

Old Texas was played for the first time at a cattlemen's association meeting in Denver, Colorado.

Texas Perspective
Charles and Molly Goodnight saved the South Plains buffalo from becoming extinct by keeping their own herd.

Charles had other pursuits besides ranching. During his life he also launched several banks, started two newspapers, and even founded two churches.

25

CROSSBREEDING

In his later years, Charles worked to improve some species of animals and plants. He did this by crossbreeding to produce hardier offspring. On his home ranch Goodnight experimented in growing hardier crops, such as wheat, by crossing different varieties. He also crossbred flowers, such as lilies, to produce different colors.

He also crossbred different species of cattle, such as the Hereford cattle and the Texas longhorns, to produce hardy cattle that could survive Texas's climate and terrain and produce good beef for people to eat. Charles also crossed buffalo with cattle to produce a new species called "cattalo." He did this to see if he could combine the good qualities of the buffalo with longhorn cattle to make even sturdier stock.

Charles Goodnight:

It has been my aim through life to try to have the world a little better because I lived in it.

This photo shows what is believed to be the last time Charles Goodnight ever rode a horse.

Today, over 3,000 buffalo, some of them descendants of the Goodnights' herd, roam freely in Yellowstone National Park.

BUFFALO TODAY

Charles and Molly saved the Southern Plains buffalo from becoming extinct. They did this by saving abandoned buffalo calves and raising their own herd of over 200 buffalo on their ranch. In fact, buffalo descended from their herd still survive to this day. During his lifetime, Charles donated some of his buffalo to zoos in New York and Europe and to Yellowstone National Park. In 1997, the Goodnight Southern Plains buffalo herd was moved to Caprock Canyons State Park near Quitaque, Texas, where they can be seen today. These surviving buffalo from the Goodnight herd are believed to be the last Southern Plains buffalo on Earth.

Molly Goodnight died in April 1926. Charles Goodnight died in December 1929. Both Charles and Molly are buried at Goodnight, Texas.

6 CHARLES'S LEGACY

Charles Goodnight was considered to be the **ideal** Texas cowman and rancher. Many Texas cattlemen drove their herds to market on the Goodnight-Loving Trail.

PRESERVING NATURE

Charles loved nature. He was known for his keen interest in the plants and animals that were native to the Llano Estacado of Texas. While working outdoors as a rancher and cattleman, he observed all kinds of animals, and learned a lot about how they behaved. Many people came to see the native Texas Panhandle animals such as elk, buffalo, and antelope, that were kept on Goodnight's ranch.

Charles Goodnight:

"All in all, my years on the trail were the happiest I ever lived. There were many hardships and dangers, of course, that called on all a man had of endurance and bravery. But when all went well, there was no other life so pleasant."

This statue of Charles Goodnight is found outside the Panhandle-Plains Historical Museum in Canyon, Texas.

GOODNIGHT, TEXAS

In 1887, Charles Goodnight bought land and built a ranch house at the edge of the Llano Estacado. Soon afterward, a railway station, post office, blacksmith shop, and school were built in the community. The town was named Goodnight, after its **founder**.

This postcard advertises the new town of Goodnight, Texas.

▲ *This photograph shows the town of Goodnight, Texas, as it looked over 100 years ago.*

GOODNIGHT TRAIL

Tourists today can travel the 12-mile-long (19 km) long Charles Goodnight Memorial Trail that begins at the Panhandle-Plains Museum, in Canyon, Texas. Goodnight used the trail to herd about 1,600 cattle from Colorado to Palo Duro Canyon in Texas in 1876. Along the trail is the **restored** dugout believed to be Charles and Molly Goodnight's first home in the Texas Panhandle.

The Charles Goodnight Memorial Trail allows visitors to retrace the steps made by Goodnight in 1876.

29

CHARLES GOODNIGHT HISTORICAL CENTER

The Charles Goodnight Historical Center opened in the fall of 2012. The Goodnights' 1887 home and surrounding land were donated so that they could be restored and used for a historical center. At the cost of about $3 million the home has been restored through the Armstrong County Museum. A visitor and education center has also been built on the site.

Buffalo roam outside the Charles Goodnight Historical Center in Goodnight, Texas. The buffalo are direct offspring of the herd that Charles and Molly raised.

LEARNING MORE

BOOKS

James, Trisha. *Cattle and Oil: The Growth of Texas Industries*. New York: The Rosen Publishing Group, 2010.

HISTORIC SITES

Armstrong County Museum
www.armstrongcountymuseum.com

Charles Goodnight Historical Center
www.armstrongcountymuseum.com/goodnight-historical-center.html

WEBSITES

The Handbook of Texas Online
www.tshaonline.org/handbook

JA Ranch
www.jaranch.org

PBS—Charles Goodnight
www.pbs.org/weta/thewest/people/d_h/goodnight.htm

TIMELINE

1823 — Military force called the Texas Rangers is formed by Stephen Austin.

1836 — Charles Goodnight is born in Macoupin County, Illinois, on March 5, 1836.

1845 — Moves to Milam County, Texas, with family.

1857 — Moves to Palo Pinto County and creates the Black Springs Ranch with stepbrother, John Sheek. Serves as scout and guide for Texas Rangers. Meets rancher Oliver Loving for first time.

1861 — On March 1, Texas joins the Confederate States of America. The Civil War begins on April 12.

1866 — Begins first cattle drive from Texas to Colorado on June 6 with Oliver Loving. Blazes new trail called the Goodnight-Loving Trail. Creates the first chuck wagon.

1867 — Oliver Loving dies.

1869 — Starts Rock Canyon Ranch in Pueblo, Colorado.

1870 — Marries Mary Ann (Molly) Dyer.

1870 — United States government encourages the killing of large numbers of wild buffalo to put in railroad tracks and save grazing lands for farm animals.

1870 — Molly Goodnight begins her own herd of Southern Plains buffalo.

1876 — Stakes a claim for land in the Palo Duro Canyon, in Texas Panhandle.

1877 — Agrees to build and manage JA Ranch for John Adair.

1878 — Makes a treaty with Comanche Indians that allows them two cattle every day until they find buffalo to hunt.

1880 — Forms the Panhandle Stock Association (PSA) and is elected president of the organization.

1882 — Puts up first barbed wire fence in Texas Panhandle. PSA gives money to begin first public school in Texas Panhandle.

1885 — John Adair dies.

1886 — Joins Northwest Texas Cattle Raisers Association.

1887 — Quits management of the JA Ranch and receives Quitaque Ranch. Buys Goodnight Ranch in Armstrong County, Texas.

1898 — Opens the Goodnight College with wife, Molly.

December 12, 1929 — Charles Goodnight dies.

Texas | Charles Goodnight

GLOSSARY

amputated (AM-pyuh-tayt-ed) Cut off or removed, especially the removal of a limb by surgery.
bankrupt (BANGK-rupt) Unable to pay the debts one owes to others.
blaze (BLAYZ) To mark out or clear a new trail.
branded (BRAND-ed) Marked with a design burned on by a hot iron pole.
crossbreed (KROS-breed) To have two or more living things with different features produce young.
earmarked (EER-markd) Cut or made a permanent mark on the ear of an animal to show ownership.
extinction (ek-STINGK-shun) The state of no longer existing.
fatal (FAY-tul) Ending in death.
founder (FOWN-dur) The person who starts something, such as a town or club.
frontier (frun-TEER) The edge of a settled country, where the wilderness begins.
gangrene (GANG-green) The death of soft tissue in a specific area of the body, due to the loss of blood.
ideal (eye-DEEL) A perfect example.
kidnapped (KID-napt) Carried off a person by force.
mustang (MUHS-tang) A wild horse descended from horses brought to North America by the Spanish.
restored (rih-STORD) Put back or returned to an earlier state.
siege (SEEJ) A strong attack.
slaughter (SLAH-ter) To kill in large numbers.
terrain (tuh-RAYN) A piece of land or the physical qualities of a piece of land.
treaty (TREE-tee) An official agreement, signed and agreed upon by each party.
tuition (tuh-WIH-shun) The price of instruction at a school.

INDEX

Adair, Cornelia 16–17
Adair, John 16–17
alkali ponds 13
Austin, Stephen 8
barbed wire fencing 23
birth place 6
Black Springs Ranch 7, 10–11
branding cattle 10
buffalo 6, 16, 18–22, 25–28, 30
Caddo Jake 6
cattalo 16, 20, 26
cattle drives 4–5, 10–12, 14–15, 22
Charles Goodnight Historical Center 30
Charles Goodnight Memorial Trail 29
childhood 6
chuck wagon 14–15
Civil War 9–11
Comanche 8–9, 12, 15, 20, 25
cowmen 10–12, 14–15, 17–18, 21
crossbreeding 18, 26
Daugherty, Hiram 6
Denver, Colorado 4, 12, 25
earmarking 10
Goodnight, Molly 16, 20–22, 24–25, 27, 29–30
Goodnight, Texas 27, 29–30
Goodnight College 24
Goodnight-Loving Trail 5, 12, 28
Goodnight Ranch 21–22
JA Ranch 16–18, 21
jockey 6
Llano Estacado 4, 13, 24, 28–29
Loving, Oliver 4–5, 11–12, 14–15
Mustang 6
Old Texas 25
Panhandle Stock Association (PSA) 21, 23
Parker, Cynthia Ann 9, 20
Parker, Quanah 20
Pecos River 4, 12
Peta Nocona 9
poisonous water holes 4, 12
Rock Canyon Ranch 16
Rocky Mountains 12
rustlers 10, 21, 23
scouting 8
Sheek, John Wesley 7
shorthorn cattle 18
slavery 9
Spaniards 7
Texas longhorn cattle 7, 18–20, 26, 28
Texas National Guard 9
Texas Rangers 8–9, 12
tracking skills 6, 9
treaty 19
vaqueros 7
Yellowstone National Park 27

32

```
+           Friends of the
B G653P    Houston Public Library
Peppas, Lynn.
Why Charles Goodnight
matters to Texas /
Central BIOGRAPHY
12/14
```